A Biography of General

Charles de Gaulle

"I Am France"

Nancy Whitelaw

A People in Focus Book

DILLON PRESS
New York

Maxwell Macmillan Canada
Toronto

Maxwell Macmillan International
New York Oxford Singapore Sydney

For Kathy, Patty, Greg, and Brad—with love

Photographic Acknowledgments

The photographs are reproduced through the courtesy of the French Embassy Press and information division.

Library of Congress Cataloging-in-Publication Data
Whitelaw, Nancy.
   Charles de Gaulle, I am France / by Nancy Whitelaw.
     p. cm. — (A People in focus book)
   Includes bibliographical references (p.   ) and index.
   Summary: A biography of the French war hero and leader.
   ISBN 0-87518-486-3
   1. Gaulle, Charles de, 1890-1970—Juvenile literature.
   2. Presidents—France—Biography—Juvenile literature. 3. Generals—France—
Biography—Juvenile literature. 4. France. Armée—Biography—Juvenile literature.
[1. Gaulle, Charles de, 1890-1970. 2. Presidents—France. 3.Generals.]
   I. Title. II. Series.
   DC420. W52 1991
   944.083' 6' 092—dc20   91-13095
   [B]

Dillon Press
Macmillan Publishing Company
866 Third Avenue
New York, NY 10022

Maxwell Macmillan Canada, Inc.
1200 Eglinton Avenue East
Suite 200
Don Mills, Ontario M3C 3N1

Macmillan Publishing Company is part of the Maxwell Communication Group of Companies.

First edition
Printed in the United States of America
10   9   8   7   6   5   4   3   2   1

Contents

Charles de Gaulle leaves the Arc de Triomphe and marches down the Champs-Elysées on August 26, 1944.

Chapter/One

I Am France

On August 26, 1944, General Charles de Gaulle returned to his beloved city of Paris. As if there were no danger, he walked slowly and proudly from the Arc de Triomphe to Notre Dame Cathedral. He waved his long arms to the cheering crowds that lined the sidewalks and reached out to touch him.

He knew that somewhere in those crowds were men who had come to kill him. Some were Germans who wanted to continue their four-year control of the city. Others were French citizens who wanted to be the ruler of France as much as the general did.

Just as de Gaulle reached Cathedral Square, shots rang out. People screamed, ran, pushed and shoved, and threw themselves flat on the ground. General de Gaulle paid no attention. As though he could neither see nor hear the panic around him, he continued his slow, majestic walk. Without a backward glance, he entered the cathedral and made the sign of the cross.

In the church, he appeared unaware of several more gunshots. He thanked God for the liberation of Paris from the Germans. He prayed for the wisdom to lead the French people to overthrow the German leaders who controlled most of the rest of the country.

After the mass, he left the cathedral to pursue the dream he had cherished for forty years. He would become the ruler of his beloved France. He had held this dream as a student in military school and as a soldier in the First World War. During the 1920s and 1930s, he had studied government procedures as he worked in several different federal offices. When Germany took over France in 1940, he created Free France, a government ready to take over as soon as the Germans were forced to retreat.

Charles de Gaulle was fifty-four years old when he became president of France. As president, he was both loved and hated, admired and criticized, respected and feared. Many foreign political leaders objected to his stubborn insistence that he and France were always right, and many French citizens also resented his superior attitude. But no one doubted that Charles de Gaulle dedicated himself completely to what he thought was best for his country.

Throughout his presidency, he used the powers of his office to build a strong France, a country that offered its citizens the freedom to live and work in security and prosperity. More than that, he wanted the best of everything for his people. "To my mind," he said, "France cannot be France without greatness."

Charles André Joseph Marie de Gaulle was born in Lille, France, on November 22, 1890, at his mother's family home. Charles and his mother soon returned to their home in Paris. The country was at peace then, although Germany retained control of the eastern provinces of Alsace and Lorraine, which it had seized in the Franco-Prussian War of 1870-1871.

Painters and sculptors, playwrights and novelists, philosophers and poets met in Paris, the political capital of France and the cultural capital of the world. There, in the 1880s, Gustave Eiffel had designed the world's largest structure, the Eiffel Tower, on the banks of the Seine River. The entire city had prepared a spectacular display, the Paris Exhibition, for the World's Fair of 1889. The grand fair attracted visitors from all over the world.

From an early age, Charles was taught to love and respect both Paris and his country. His father, Henri de Gaulle, had served as a colonel in 1870 in the Franco-Prussian War, in which France had been defeated. Every year Monsieur de Gaulle took his family to the

The house in Lille in the north of France where Charles de Gaulle was born on November 22, 1890.

battlefield at Le Bourget to read the inscription on the monument to those who died there: "The sword of France, broken in their valiant hands, will be forged again by their descendants." Charles was proud to think of himself as a descendant who would pick up the sword of France.

In so doing, he would carry on family tradition. Through the centuries, men of the de Gaulle family had repeatedly proven their bravery. In 1210, Richard de Gaulle fought against the English. In the 1400s, another de Gaulle saved his town from invaders, and still another defended the gates of Paris against the Duke of Burgundy. In the eighteenth century, during the French Revolution, Jean Baptiste de Gaulle refused to renounce his loyalty to the French king. Rebels who seized control of the government imprisoned him for his faithfulness to the crown.

Although no real battles were fought in Paris when Charles was growing up, war was his favorite game. He and his three brothers often pretended to be soldiers in battles that they had read about in history books. When Xavier, Charles, Jacques, and Pierre acted out wars in which France had been defeated, Charles changed history. When Charles played, France always won. In their games, Charles refused to play if he could not take the part of France. When the other children asked why, he replied, "Because *I* am France, that's why!"

Sometimes he and his brothers played indoors with tiny tin soldiers. They set them up in battalions. The scarlet-coated officers on white horses led troops of infantry soldiers holding drawn bayonets.

Sometimes they played war with gangs of boys in the fields.

Charles' main interest was in the strategy, making and carrying out plans. He used strategy the way a football coach does—drilling his men, studying his opponents, experimenting with different formations, planning attacks, and preparing defenses.

Charles drew up the plans, and he expected the others to follow his orders. One day he gave his little brother Pierre a secret message and told him to swallow the note if he were captured. Pierre was captured, but he gave up the note to the enemy instead of swallowing it.

Charles slapped him. Pierre ran home crying, "General Charles slapped me." Charles explained to his mother that he was forced to punish Pierre because he had disobeyed orders.

Sometimes Charles liked to pretend that he was General Napoleon Bonaparte, a brilliant French leader who ruled France in the early 1800s. Bonaparte had said that he would never be afraid because he had faith in his special "star." Charles thought that he, too, had a star that protected him. Once when he was sliding down a bannister, he did not turn sharply enough and crashed onto the floor. His mother rushed to him, afraid that he had been seriously hurt. Charles told her she should never worry about him, because he had a star just like the one Napoleon had.

Besides this belief that he was especially protected by a star, Charles had a deep religious faith. Every night Jeanne de Gaulle, a devout Catholic, listened as her children said their prayers for blessings on themselves, their families, and their country. Sometimes Charles prayed to the statue of the Virgin Mary that adorned a building directly outside his bedroom window. Often Jeanne told her children stories of religious heroes.

Charles' home life was rather quiet. Mealtimes were usually serious occasions. After Henri de Gaulle said grace, no one spoke until everyone had finished the meal, which was usually a simple stew or soup. Then Henri, who taught philosophy, mathematics, and literature, would begin nightly teaching sessions at home for the four boys and their sister, Marie-Agnès. The children were expected to prepare themselves for these after-dinner lessons.

Henri might ask his children to describe their meal in Latin or in classical Greek, to work out a problem in geometry, or to listen while he gave a science lecture. Sometimes he led them in discussions and arguments about history, philosophy, and literature. When Charles disagreed with an opinion, he used his favorite expression, "That's absurd."

After the lessons, each family member worked on his own project. The children sat at the dining room table to do their homework while their mother knitted or embroidered and their father corrected papers.

Although Charles took his lessons seriously, he was not always serious about words. He made up a game of pronouncing words backwards. He called this game "Siaçnarf," which is "français" (French) backwards. He called himself "Selrahc ed Elluag." After much practice, he became quick at reading backwards, and he even memorized whole pages that way, just for fun.

The first school that Charles attended was a Jesuit school, the College of the Immaculate Conception in Paris. There discipline was strict, and students were expected to study hard. Every Saturday their grades were read aloud for everyone to hear. Charles' grades in mathematics were so high that his professors suggested that he study business. Charles was not interested. He had already made up his mind to go to the famous French military school, Saint-Cyr, and to become a soldier. His parents were pleased with this decision. Charles' school was closed in 1905 under a law that prohibited the church from owning property. The de Gaulles wanted him to continue his Jesuit education, so they sent him to a Jesuit school in Belgium.

Charles as a grade-school student.

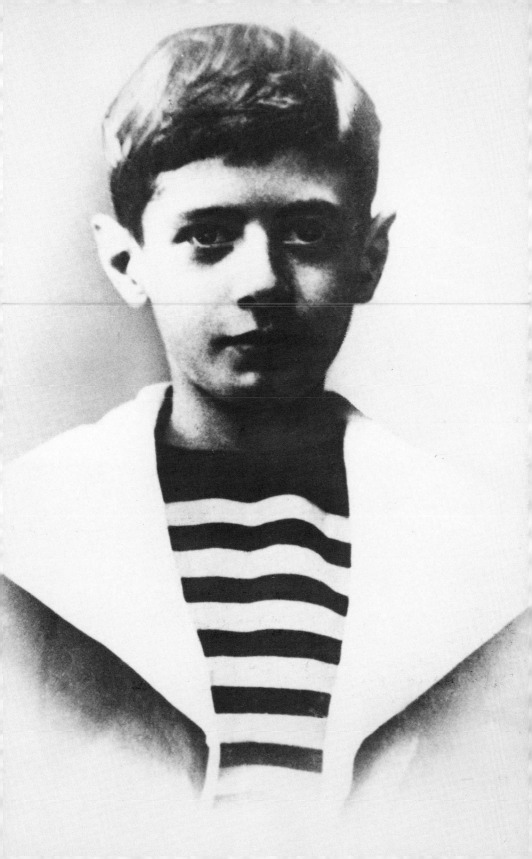

When he was fourteen years old, he wrote a play about a bandit and a traveler. He entered this play in a writing contest and won first prize. Although he was pleased, Charles worried that his parents would be angry. They had warned him that he should spend more time on his studies and less time on reading and writing for fun. His prize was fifty copies of the play, and he hid them away in a closet. His mother found them, and she told Charles that he should be proud, not ashamed, of his writing.

In 1908, his father felt that Charles' background in science and math was weak. He enrolled him in Stanislas College in Paris to prepare for the stiff entrance exam he would need to take to get into Saint-Cyr.

A year later, at the age of nineteen, Charles had to meet another requirement for entrance to the military school. Each Saint-Cyr student was required to spend a year as a common soldier before he began formal schooling. The school required this so that students would learn how to obey before they learned how to command. In 1909, Charles joined the Thirty-third Infantry Regiment at Arras, near his birthplace of Lille.

Nineteen-year-old Private de Gaulle was almost six and a half feet tall, and his bony wrists and ankles stuck out beyond his sleeves and trouser legs. His long neck protruded out of the tight collar of his jacket. "Like a plant," said the other young men, "just like an asparagus plant." From them on, Charles was nicknamed The Big Asparagus.

Long arms, long legs, long neck—Charles even had a long nose! The other soldiers said he resembled Cyrano de Bergerac, a character in the play *Cyrano de Bergerac*. They made him sing the hero's song:

> How do you drink with such a nose?
> You ought to have a cup made specially...

They also laughed at his cold personality, saying that he must have been brought up in an icehouse. The more they teased, the more he withdrew. He rarely spoke to anyone.

When he did speak, it was usually to criticize some of the military regulations. He was quick to point out that he thought inspections and drills were a waste of his time. His interest was in military strategy, not in discipline and physical training.

He frequently disobeyed orders and had to march extra turns around the parade ground with a heavy pack and a rifle. Although many cadets won stripes for good behavior, Charles did not earn a single one. His instructors believed that he did not even try to obey military rules and regulations. "It makes no difference to him," one of them said. "That one thinks he's already a general."

Although his record as an infantry soldier was poor, Charles entered Saint-Cyr in 1910 at the age of twenty. There he criticized his superiors just as he had in the infantry. During lectures, his classmates often heard him mutter, "That is absurd."

That was his comment when his professors scoffed at airplanes, calling them useless, flimsy things. Charles repeated it when the instructors said that machine guns consumed too much ammunition to be useful. He repeated it when he was told that Germany would never again threaten France, as it had during the Franco-Prussian War.

One professor became Charles' hero. Colonel Henri Philippe Pétain continually criticized the military strategies of the other instructors and of the French General Staff, the military leaders of France. The professor and his favorite student met often to discuss military matters. They agreed that their leaders lacked imagination and vision: "We're commanded by grocers."

The two men disagreed with the General Staff theory of attack. This strategy focused on old-fashioned bayonets and the bravery of individual soldiers. Pétain and de Gaulle recommended the use of modern machine guns and other heavy artillery before engaging in man-to-man fighting.

Despite his disagreements with professors, Charles

Twenty-one-year-old de Gaulle as a Saint-Cyr cadet in 1910-1911.

earned high grades at Saint-Cyr and graduated in the top ten percent of his class. On October 1, 1912, he became Second Lieutenant de Gaulle. He chose to return to his old Thirty-third Infantry Regiment, where Colonel Pétain had become commanding officer.

Chapter/Two

The Divine Game of Heroes

At Arras, de Gaulle and Pétain were not equals in military rank, but they respected each other as equals in military knowledge. The two soldiers spent long hours together, devising strategy for an army that existed only in their dreams. They pretended that the French army was equipped with machine guns, tanks, and air power. They created battle scenes, and they devised plans for offensive and defensive action, such as the ten-year-old Charles had done with his toy soldiers.

They cornered men in dining halls and recreation areas and tried to lecture to them about the importance of reequipping and retraining French soldiers. They pointed out that German Kaiser Wilhelm II's soldiers were positioning guns and cannons to aim straight at France. The officers were not interested. They believed that Pétain and de Gaulle were just enjoying an extension of children's war games.

Then a chain of international events and reactions to events caused World War I. One of the most significant events was an assassination that occurred on July 28, 1914. Archduke Francis Ferdinand, the man who seemed most likely to become the next ruler of Austria, was killed. The Austrians blamed the Serbs and immediately began preparing for war against them. Serbia's neighbors, the Russians, sent in troops to protect them from the Austrians. Germans took advantage of the unrest to plan attacks on France.

Unlike most French citizens, Charles de Gaulle did not panic when the sound of heavy German artillery awoke Parisians one morning shortly after the German invasion of Belgium. He had predicted the attack, and he was ready to defend his country. To him combat was "the divine game of heroes," and he did not deny that he was looking forward to the battles.

Lieutenant de Gaulle knew the name and service record of each man under him, and he was as proud of his troops as they were of him. They were an impressive unit, these young officers in their bright red coats and shiny brass buttons and their spotless white gloves. Their rifles gleamed, and the white plumes of their tall hats waved in the breeze as they advanced in orderly rows, ready to battle the Germans.

But the Germans were not advancing toward the enemy in orderly rows. They were hiding in trenches, waiting and watching. As their targets moved closer, Germans slid down, steadying the barrels of their guns on the rims of the trenches. At a signal, they opened fire, and the front line of French soldiers was demolished. Another line advanced, and German bullets went tearing into them. Over and over again, the pattern continued.

Riding at the head of his regiment, de Gaulle was a model of courage for his troops. Many soldiers ducked as bullets whizzed by, or they threw themselves on the ground as bayonets were thrust at them. But Lieutenant Charles de Gaulle pushed forward, erect and fearless, until suddenly, on August 15, 1914, he was wounded. He described the event in his journal:

> I had just covered the last twenty meters
> to the bridge when I felt what seemed to
> be a whiplash on my knee, and I missed my
> footing....A hail of bullets hit the pavement
> and walls around us and thumped with a duller
> sound into the dead and wounded on the ground.

In the hospital, he was a headstrong patient, continually insisting that he was needed back on the battlefield. After seven months, he left the infirmary against the doctors' advice. A month later, a piece of shrapnel tore into his left hand, and he was back in the hospital for another five months.

Again he argued that he was needed on the battlefield. Not strong enough to engage in combat, he asked to use his knowledge of the German language to act as a spy. Soon de Gaulle was back in the middle of the fighting, crawling in and out of mud-filled trenches and sliding under barbed wire. He brought back important news of German troop movements and plans. French soldiers began to repeat stories about this fearless lieutenant who continued to risk his life for his country.

Just as in military school, de Gaulle spent hours arguing with his superiors. Over and over, he tried to convince them that French soldiers were being forced to commit suicide as they marched straight into German lines. He begged them to look at the record—in 1915, on the French front alone, over 1,300,000 French soldiers were killed, wounded, or taken prisoner, and only 500,000 Germans were put out of action.

In January 1915, he was sent to the Verdun front in eastern France. Over 315,000 French troops had been killed there in just six months. The commanding officer wrote: "In view of the gravity of the situation...I believe that de Gaulle alone is capable of accomplishing it."

The newly promoted captain rushed to Douaumont

Captain de Gaulle in 1915.

near Verdun. During a battle, a German soldier thrust a bayonet into his thigh. De Gaulle fell.

His fellow soldiers reported that he had been killed in action. Pétain declared that de Gaulle was "an officer without equal in every respect," and that he had earned the Legion of Honor Cross.

Charles de Gaulle was not dead. He was found by a German soldier and taken to a hospital on a stretcher. When he recovered, he was taken to a prisoner-of-war camp. While there he insisted that soldiers salute and use proper military titles when they spoke to each other. He kept his uniform as immaculate as possible. Perhaps most important, he insisted that all war talk focus on the triumph of French forces over the enemy.

De Gaulle obeyed the French military code that dictated that prisoners should try to escape. Once he sneaked outside the prison walls in a supply cart, but he was caught by a sentry. A short time later, he sneaked away again, but that time he was caught by police dogs. Another time, he stole a German officer's uniform. He was quickly identified since the sleeves did not cover his long arms, and the pants did not reach his ankles.

It became clear that Charles de Gaulle would never stop trying to escape. He was transferred to Fort Nine on the Danube River, a prison for particularly difficult captives. There he was greeted by a hundred French, British, and Russian prisoners who sang the French national anthem, the "Marseillaise," to greet this well-known prisoner-of-war.

Fort Nine was a stone fortress surrounded by fifty-foot-wide moats. Heavily armed guards with spiked helmets and fixed bayonets patrolled the gates day and night. De Gaulle tried to escape twice, but he was quickly caught both times. His punishment was 120 days in solitary confinement. There he spent long, lonely hours reciting Greek poetry to himself.

After the solitary confinement, de Gaulle lived with nine other men in a ten-by-forty-foot room. Two barred windows and a single electric light bulb supplied the only light. A coal stove served for both cooking and heating. De Gaulle spent hours with the only reading material available, German newspapers.

Thousands of miles away, the American people were debating about entering the war against Germany. The Germans restricted the travel of American ships. In vain, United States president Woodrow Wilson attempted to reach a peaceful settlement with Germany.

On April 2, 1917, Wilson asked Congress to declare war on Germany. By October of the following year, over 1,750,000 American soldiers had come to France to fight. The Germans surrendered in November. That same month, just before his twenty-eighth birthday, de Gaulle was released from the prison camp.

By the time the peace conference began in Versailles,

France, de Gaulle was once again a soldier—this time in the Polish army. He regretted that he had been out of action for more than half the war because of his wounds and his capture. He eagerly applied for more military service when Poland recruited servicemen in a conflict against the Bolsheviks, the Russian communists who were threatening to take over Poland.

After the Poles were victorious, de Gaulle was awarded the highest Polish military decoration. He considered accepting a position as instructor in a Polish war college, but something happened when he was home in Paris on leave. De Gaulle fell in love.

Chapter / Three

The Important Thing Is to Make One's Mark

In 1920, de Gaulle attended an art exhibition in Paris while on leave from Poland. There he met Yvonne Vendroux, a handsome young woman with dark hair. He did not know that Yvonne came from a family of well-to-do biscuit makers from Calais. They had engaged the services of a matchmaker for their daughter. This woman arranged the meeting and reported, "I introduced Charles to Yvonne, and they immediately walked ahead alone, talking about the paintings."

Charles was seldom comfortable in social situations, and this one was no exception. He sat on a fragile gilded chair next to Yvonne, trying to balance his cap, his gloves, and a dainty cup and saucer on his bony knees. The balancing act did not succeed. He spilled tea onto her lap. Embarrassed, he apologized.

The next day he went to her home with a bouquet of flowers and a second apology. After that, he visited Yvonne frequently. Apparently, it was love at first sight for both of them.

They met again at a fancy dress ball, and they danced six waltzes together. Then Yvonne spoke to her brother, who was with her. "Captain de Gaulle has asked me to marry him. I said yes."

De Gaulle had to return to Poland to fulfill his military commitment there. However, a few months later, he was offered an appointment as a lecturer at Saint-Cyr, and he eagerly accepted the opportunity to return to Paris.

In April 1921, Charles de Gaulle and Yvonne Vendroux were married at the church of Notre Dame de Calais near the English Channel. They drove to the church in a hired carriage. The groom asked the coachmen to wear the blue, white, and red colors of the French flag as decorations on their top hats.

Charles and Madame de Gaulle settled down in a small apartment in Paris. The new bride admitted that she had no interest in military life, but she promised to be a loyal wife and to support her husband in every decision. She believed that her duty was to look after the men and children in her family. She and her husband seldom participated in the social life around them. Instead, they preferred to enjoy each other's company.

They also spent happy weekends at Yvonne's family home, where Charles often rode horses. That winter their first child, Philippe, was born.

At Saint-Cyr, Professor de Gaulle became well known for his flair for the dramatic. When he lectured about France's defeat in the Franco-Prussian War, he asked the class to stand at attention out of respect for the eternal spirit of the French Army. According to one of his students, "It was almost as if he actually lived through the centuries of history he lectured about."

A fellow teacher once said to de Gaulle, "I have a curious feeling that you are pledged to a great destiny." Perhaps he was surprised when de Gaulle, after a moment's thought, agreed.

As part of his work at Saint-Cyr, de Gaulle was assigned to the École Supérieure de Guerre, a school for military officers, where he studied military strategy. He was as quick to question and criticize his teachers there as he had been at Saint-Cyr. One report said of him: "Could achieve excellent results if he admitted mistakes with a little better grace, and if he consented more easily to allow his point of view to be disputed."

In the annual war games at the school, de Gaulle's troops faced the troops of the school director. De Gaulle knew that the opposing team would stand together, creating a heavy line of fire that his troops could not penetrate. He divided his regiment into small groups. These groups used shoot-and-run tactics that confused and finally defeated the stronger troops. The director flew into a fit of rage and accused de Gaulle of unfair tactics. De Gaulle replied with just two words: "I won."

Perhaps he was punished for this victory. De Gaulle felt that he was. When he graduated, he did not receive the hoped-for assignment to the General Staff to work with military strategy. Instead, he was assigned to the Army of the Rhine in Mayence, where he worked with refrigeration, supplies, and transportation.

He left school in a fit of temper, declaring, "I will come back to this dirty hole only when I am commandant of it."

While in Mayence, he further angered his superiors by publishing a book, *La discorde chez l'ennemi (Conflicts among the Enemy)*, a series of essays on the 1918-1919 collapse of Germany. They were displeased because soldiers were not supposed to write for publication unless they were assigned to do so. Charles de Gaulle had given himself the assignment. He justified his actions by declaring that French military and political leaders needed to understand the situation as he saw it.

In 1925, Pétain ordered de Gaulle back to Paris to write another book—this one about the need for a strong national military force. De Gaulle was glad to be with Yvonne, Philippe, and his first daughter, Elisabeth, in his beloved city, with its broad tree-shaded streets and green parks. As often as he had time, de Gaulle took his children for walks down the city streets and over some of the thirty-two graceful bridges that spanned the Seine River as it flowed through the city. He wanted his children to share his love of Paris.

When he was promoted and called back to a command post in 1927, he scoffed, "It is nice to be promoted, but the real question is different. The important thing is to make one's mark." The new major's assignment was to command a light infantry unit in the Rhineland at Trèves. There he made his mark by breaking tradition about military berets (soft, simple hats worn by soldiers). De Gaulle ordered his troops to wear theirs slanted to the right, the opposite of all the other troops. He gave no reason and allowed no argument about the matter.

He made his mark another time when he insisted on bringing his troops back to the base camp after field maneuvers. He refused to accept the opinion of a military doctor that the weather was too harsh for the trip. De Gaulle was not asking his troops to do anything he would not do. He marched at the head of the unit as he led them back.

Although his troops knew him as a demanding military commander, his family knew de Gaulle as a loving husband and father. He was especially sympathetic toward their third child, Anne, who was retarded. At her birth, he said, "She did not ask to come into the world. We shall do everything possible to make her happy." He spent many hours with this beloved child, playing with her, talking to her, and doing tricks to make her laugh.

His family moved to Beirut, Lebanon, with him when he asked for and received an assignment in the Middle East. He wanted to see for himself if the French colonies in Cairo, Damascus, Aleppo, and Jerusalem maintained strong patriotic ties to France and if they would be important allies in case of war. At the end of his two-year appointment, he reported that France should either assert stronger control over the colonies or grant them complete independence. De Gaulle believed in forceful control or none at all.

Returning to France in 1932, the de Gaulle family again settled down in Paris. Charles was appointed to the National Defense Council, a committee assigned to establish French military security. Once again, he had hopes that he could convince political and military leaders to build a stronger military force.

During this time, de Gaulle wrote two more books. One was *Le fil de l'épée (The Edge of the Sword)*, a study of military leadership. He also wrote *Vers l'armée de métier*, which was published in English as *The Army of the Future*. This book outlined his plan to achieve military strength. De Gaulle was frustrated that French military leaders paid no attention to it.

The book might have been forgotten except that some German leaders took an interest in it. These leaders made the book required reading for military personnel. De Gaulle's plans for strengthening the French army were widely discussed by the Nazis, the political group that had seized power in Germany in 1933.

These Nazis, under their leader Adolf Hitler, were creating a strong army as they prepared to add land and people to their empire. The Italians joined them, under their leader Mussolini, and the two powers became known as the Axis. On September 1, 1939, German soldiers invaded Poland, chanting: "Today we rule Germany, tomorrow the whole world."

De Gaulle wrote secretly to eighty different political officials, begging them to support a program to build armored tanks and to allow him to lead a regiment against the Germans. At that moment, the Nazi army was pushing through Belgium. Few officials responded.

One who did was Paul Reynaud, a cabinet member. Reynaud could not grant his requests, but he did persuade de Gaulle to help him in his political campaign to become premier of France. During this campaign, de Gaulle learned firsthand about problems in the French system of government.

Because there were so many political parties, no single party could achieve a majority in the National Assembly, a legislative body of elected officials. Representatives in the assembly were more interested in their own districts than in the nation as a whole. De Gaulle compared the system to an army with hundreds of generals, each serving one small unit and none serving the country. Often, important legislative matters were stalled in the assembly because members would not negotiate an agreement. When this happened, the prime minister or sometimes members of the assembly would call for new elections. They hoped that different representatives would be able to coordinate their efforts better. This "vote of no confidence" occurred six times between 1932 and 1934. The result was that few government officials were in office long enough to pass legislation.

While the French government faltered, the Germans continued their westward march. As de Gaulle had predicted, sixteen armored Nazi divisions advanced from Belgium into northern France. They quickly defeated the four weak French divisions stationed there. At last the French High Command gave de Gaulle permission to take military action.

Chapter / Four

The Flame of Resistance Must Not Die

De Gaulle was ready. By May 15, 1940, he was leading an armored regiment in a suburb of Paris. He had requested five hundred tanks, several regiments of infantry troops, and protective air power to fight the advancing Nazi army. He had received only twenty tanks and no other equipment. Still he declared, "If I live, I will fight...until the enemy is defeated and the national honor washed clean." As a symbol of patriotism, he chose the cross of Lorraine, a double-barred cross that had been Joan of Arc's emblem five hundred years before. Although his troops fought bravely, half of the regiment was killed in just four days.

Charles, newly promoted to brigadier general, wrote to Yvonne: "I spent your birthday in the thick of the fight....I thought of you and sent you my loving wishes, Yvonne." He added that he was disappointed that Philippe and Elisabeth, both away at school, did not write to him. In another letter, he wrote to Yvonne: "Everybody here says to me: 'We hope your wife wasn't too upset by the opening of the campaign.' I reply with the truth, which is 'No'; but I think to myself that perhaps she *was* upset, but had the courage to pretend not to be...."

As the German soldiers approached Paris, French citizens panicked. Seven million refugees and two million retreating soldiers clogged the roads to the south—traveling in trucks, cars, bicycles, fire trucks, wheelbarrows—anything that had wheels. Most had nowhere to go. They thought only of escaping from the invading Nazis.

Abruptly, Reynaud sent orders to de Gaulle to return to Paris to become under secretary for national defense. Perhaps he did not want to leave the battlefield, but de Gaulle obeyed the order of his premier. When he arrived in Paris, he learned that both his old friend Pétain and the supreme commander of French forces, General Maxime Weygand, were trying to convince Reynaud to surrender to the Germans.

De Gaulle was outraged at the mention of surrender. As his first act in his new position, he requested that British Prime Minister Winston Churchill send Royal Air Force troops to help the French continue their

Brigadier General de Gaulle in the early 1940s.

struggle. Churchill refused, saying that the British needed to keep their troops for their own defense.

Disappointed but not defeated, de Gaulle suggested moving French men and supplies to North Africa, where they could regain their strength. He had to give up his plan on June 10, 1940, when he left Paris in fear for his life. As he left, he insisted, "We must fight ... and if all is lost, we must carry on from our colonies in Africa and from the decks of our naval ships." Most other French leaders disagreed; they thought only of surrender.

On June 14, German troops marched proudly down the Champs-Elysées, the main street of the capital, with drums rolling and fifes playing. By ten o'clock in the morning, the black-and-red flags bearing the Nazi swastika—the symbol of a cross with the arms bent at right angles—flew from government buildings.

De Gaulle traveled to London for the second time to ask Churchill for help. This time, Churchill said yes, and he telephoned Reynaud to say, "De Gaulle is right! You must hold out."

But when he arrived back in Bordeaux, de Gaulle learned that Reynaud had resigned, and Pétain, the new premier, was urging the French to surrender.

De Gaulle could not sleep that night. Around midnight, he went for a walk in the silent streets. Suddenly he noticed that footsteps behind him slowed when he slowed and speeded up when he did. De Gaulle realized that he was being followed. He understood that Pétain feared he might try to start an anti-surrender movement. De Gaulle was no longer a free man in his own country.

He hastened back to his hotel where he made two important phone calls. The first was to make plans for escape the next day. The second was to ask a friend to tell Madame de Gaulle of his plans. He dared not contact her directly. Then he stuffed his important papers in a leather bag containing a spare pair of uniform trousers, four khaki shirts, and a photograph of his family.

Early the next morning, he arrived at the airport. He said that he had been assigned to escort Sir Edward Spears, a British statesman, to the plane for London. He watched as his bag, along with Spears' trunks, was loaded onto the plane. The two men shook hands, and Spears climbed aboard.

Suddenly, as de Gaulle had planned, the pilot stuck his head out of the window and asked for a rope to tie down some baggage. An agent who was in on the plan came running up with the rope, and de Gaulle grabbed it from him. He threw one end to Spears, who caught it and pulled de Gaulle into the plane. The door slammed shut, and the plane took off. De Gaulle had escaped from his own country.

General de Gaulle at the microphone of the BBC on June 18, 1940.

When he got to Britain, de Gaulle's first act was to broadcast over British (BBC) radio: "I, General de Gaulle, call on all French officers and men...to get in touch with me. Whatever happens, the flame of French resistance must not and will not die."

Charles de Gaulle announced the birth of a government called Free France and his acceptance of its leadership. He cabled orders to his homeland that citizens should refuse to surrender to the Germans. Neither soldiers nor civilians responded. They were face-to-face with the guns of the enemy, and they would

A TOUS LES FRANÇAIS

La France a perdu une bataille!
Mais la France n'a pas perdu la guerre!

Des gouvernants de rencontre ont pu capituler, cédant à la panique, oubliant l'honneur, livrant le pays à la servitude. Cependant, rien n'est perdu!

Rien n'est perdu, parce que cette guerre est une guerre mondiale. Dans l'univers libre, des forces immenses n'ont pas encore donné. Un jour, ces forces écraseront l'ennemi. Il faut que la France, ce jour-là, soit présente à la victoire. Alors, elle retrouvera sa liberté et sa grandeur. Tel est mon but, mon seul but!

Voilà pourquoi je convie tous les Français, où qu'ils se trouvent, à s'unir à moi dans l'action, dans le sacrifice et dans l'espérance.

Notre patrie est en péril de mort.
Luttons tous pour la sauver!

VIVE LA FRANCE !

TO ALL FRENCHMEN...

LONG LIVE FRANCE!

C. de Gaulle.

GÉNÉRAL DE GAULLE

QUARTIER GÉNÉRAL,
4, CARLTON GARDENS,
LONDON, S.W.1.

Posters were made of de Gaulle's June 18 BBC radio broadcast which proclaimed, "France has lost a battle! But France has not lost the war!"

not risk their lives for this little-known general, who himself had fled from the Germans. De Gaulle understood. He admitted, "For those still over there... it's a dreadful thing to decide, whether to obey orders...or to leave all, perhaps to lose all. A terrible choice!" He organized a memorial service for those loyal French citizens who were murdered as the Germans began their takeover.

At the outbreak of the war, Yvonne had fled to Brittany to be near her mother-in-law. She and Charles had agreed that she would join him in England if he was forced to go there.

Yvonne was able to board the last ship from Brest before the Germans marched in. De Gaulle's mother, now a widow, remained in Brittany with her son, Xavier. Yvonne arrived in Plymouth, England, bringing only their children and the keys to their home in France. She hastened to join Charles in London.

Yvonne de Gaulle had escaped just in time. On June 23, Pétain signed the official papers acknowledging France's surrender to Germany. He announced that France would be split into two zones.

One zone, encompassing three-fifths of the country, was to be occupied directly by the Germans. This area stretched from the German border north and east to the English Channel and south to Spain. Paris was at the heart of this zone. The rest of the country was described as "unoccupied" and was to be ruled by Pétain under German supervision. The capital of this zone was Vichy, and the zone became known as Vichy France.

One of the first moves of the Vichy government was to sentence de Gaulle to death for treason. De Gaulle scoffed. He believed that his accusers were the ones who were guilty of treason. They had surrendered; he had not.

The forty-nine-year-old general set up an office in a crowded three-room apartment, lighted by bare electric light bulbs and furnished with simple tables and chairs. Like his office, his attitude toward visitors was simple, cold, and efficient. As a military man, he expected unquestioning obedience from those below him in rank.

He greeted recruits abruptly, not like a coach trying to build a winning team, but like a personnel manager accepting job applications. Newspaper writers complained of his abruptness toward them. He began each press conference with a long speech and then left the room before they could ask more than one or two questions.

He was especially sensitive about his private life. The de Gaulles moved to a country home outside London, where Charles relaxed as often as he could on weekends. There Madame de Gaulle created a refuge

General and Madame de Gaulle in their garden at their home outside London in the early 1940s.

for her husband, and she took care of Anne. Philippe joined the Free French Navy, and Elisabeth enrolled in a school at Oxford. Sometimes de Gaulle strolled through the small English villages, arm in arm with Anne. He pretended not to hear the unkind remarks about her awkwardness.

When de Gaulle's mother died, the Germans tried to cover up the news to prevent any sympathetic outpouring for de Gaulle. But a Breton fisherman was able to smuggle a photo of Jeanne de Gaulle's grave across the Channel to her son.

News from France often angered de Gaulle, but it never discouraged him. His faith in himself and in Free France inspired others to join him. These first recruits included two hundred French soldiers who had been evacuated from Dunkirk by the British, a flotilla of fishing boats, sailors from a French submarine on the Norwegian coast, and some French airmen who had traveled from North Africa to be part of Free France. De Gaulle's message to them was brief: "So you have escaped. That is good. But what you have done is nothing. Until France is liberated, you must never stop fighting."

De Gaulle asked Churchill for money to buy arms and supplies. He promised to repay the loan in the near future when Free French troops marched triumphantly back to France. Churchill agreed.

De Gaulle insisted that British representatives sign a pledge to provide military aid for Free France and to name him, Charles de Gaulle, the Supreme Commander of Free French forces. When members of the British press accused de Gaulle of being difficult, de Gaulle answered that they were wrong. He said the problem lay with the British, who were too narrow-minded to accept new ideas.

De Gaulle's title was Supreme Commander, but

he was required to coordinate his plans with those of the British High Command. Conflict began almost immediately over two French battleships and several cruisers. The crews had escaped from the Germans, and the ships were floating in a harbor off the coast of Algeria, in northern Africa. De Gaulle wanted to take control of the ships in the name of the Free French Navy. Churchill feared that the Germans would seize them first. To prevent this, he ordered that the British sink them. From that time on, De Gaulle was suspicious about British loyalty to him. Immediately, he set up a secret intelligence bureau to gather inside information about British leaders.

Military strategy was not enough to create a country. De Gaulle also needed a body of men to be "the government" of Free France. Some French leaders who had escaped from Paris joined him now in London. He welcomed each man briefly, asking each what he had to offer to Free France and assuring him that France would soon be great again.

He requested that other countries recognize his new government. In the United States, President Franklin Roosevelt saw no reason to acknowledge this general, who had left the country he now claimed to serve. The United States recognized Pétain as the leader of France. Churchill was more cooperative, perhaps because a Free French military force in England would

King George VI and de Gaulle review Free French troops.

be valuable if the Germans attacked his country.

The Free French movement grew. In August of 1940, a parade of seven thousand Free French marched in front of King George VI of England. Infantrymen in light gray uniforms, cavalrymen with blue berets, and Foreign Legionnaires with white-visored hats marched behind General de Gaulle. Their eyes were on the French flags, decorated with the cross of Lorraine, as they proudly sang the "Marseillaise."

De Gaulle needed more than parades. To recruit more men and broader support, he traveled to French colonies in West Africa. At each stop, the Free French honor guard marched through the dusty village streets playing military marches, displaying bright flags, and wearing smart red fezzes (cone-shaped hats with black tassels). After the parade, de Gaulle asked for support for the Free French.

The routine was a success. In just a few months, he received assurance of support from African leaders in the Ivory Coast, French Equatorial Africa, Chad, the Cameroons, and Brazzaville. Although he realized that most of the Africans would never accept an assignment to fight in France, de Gaulle counted each pledge of loyalty as a victory for Free France.

With this show of new strength, he persuaded Churchill to plan a joint Free French/British attack on Vichy troops in Dakar, the capital of French West Africa. When the attack failed, General de Gaulle admitted: "I went through what a man must feel when an earthquake shakes his house brutally and he receives on his head the rain of tiles falling from the roof."

Soon his discouragement gave way to determination. Charles de Gaulle had no time for self-pity.

Chapter / Five

I Now Speak for France

On December 7, 1941, the Japanese attacked the Americans at Pearl Harbor, in Hawaii. Both the United States and Great Britain declared war on Japan. The Japanese joined forces with the Germans and the Italians, and the Axis grew. The French, Americans, Russians, and British united with over twenty smaller countries to form an opposing power, the Allies. De Gaulle felt confident that the Allies would win the war. Still, he was not confident that the Allies would help him to become leader of the French after the war.

However, de Gaulle was building support among French citizens through his work with the Resistance—an underground organization in France whose members sabotaged Nazi arms factories, blew up supply trains, created disruptions in transportation systems, and obtained useful military information for the Allies. He sent money, supplies, and trained French agents from London. Perhaps most important, de Gaulle sent his confidence in the liberation of France.

Jean Moulin was one of the most famous Resistance fighters. At two o'clock on the morning of January 1, 1942, Moulin parachuted from a British plane into a marsh in the Rhône Valley, where he landed waist-deep in the icy water. Hidden in his clothes were half a million francs and a matchbox with a secret compartment that contained a microphotograph of his orders from de Gaulle. His mission was to organize groups of Resistance fighters, to set up centers to receive arms and equipment parachuted from England, and to create a network of support for de Gaulle's return. He eluded the Gestapo—the Nazi secret police—for two and a half years before he was captured and tortured to death.

De Gaulle's brothers Xavier and Pierre and his sister Marie-Agnès and her husband were also Resistance fighters. All were arrested for spying against the Nazis, and they were sent to German concentration camps. His brother Jacques fled to Switzerland. Yvonne de Gaulle's brother and sister were also sent to concentration camps. Many Resistance fighters and French Jews died in these death camps.

De Gaulle was aware that his assignments to Resistance fighters might lead to death. "The road is a cruel one," he said, "yet this pain will not keep us from marching toward our goal, which is to restore France to her destiny." As the strength of the Resistance grew, so did the strength of the Gestapo. They arrested, jailed, tortured, and murdered anyone suspected of resistance. A million French men were shipped to Germany to work as slave laborers in the factories there. Entire French villages were destroyed by the Gestapo in retaliation against resisters.

As the Resistance grew within France, the Free French movement grew outside of the country. By 1942, three hundred thousand people had registered as supporters of de Gaulle and his movement. De Gaulle now opened his daily radio broadcasts by saying, "I, General de Gaulle, represent the legitimate government of France." With these words he authorized himself to be leader above any claims by the Nazi occupation forces or by the Vichy government.

Roosevelt and Churchill complained that de Gaulle was more interested in himself and in France than in Allied unity to end the war. Some of their criticisms seemed to please de Gaulle. Sir Anthony Eden, Britain's foreign minister, told him, "I regret to have to tell you, General, that His Majesty's government considers that it has more difficulties with Free France than with all its other allies combined."

De Gaulle smiled and answered, "I have always

told you, sir, that France is a great country."

The Allies then tried to avoid working with de Gaulle. Overlooking his popularity in North Africa, they supported the appointment of General Henri Giraud as commander in chief of the French forces there. De Gaulle was outraged, but he said nothing at the time. He would wait until he could act.

Without consulting de Gaulle, the Allies planned a top level strategy meeting in Casablanca, on the Atlantic coast of Morocco. Then they decided to invite de Gaulle in order to show the world that the Allies were a unified group. The general refused, saying that he did not accept last minute invitations. Churchill threatened to withdraw British support for the Free French if de Gaulle did not appear at the meeting.

De Gaulle did go, but he brought his own list of topics to discuss. He displayed little interest in the Allied agenda, and he repeated his demand that the Allies support him as ruler of post-war France. The Allies refused. When reporters asked for pictures, de Gaulle shook hands and smiled with the others. He was learning to play the part of a diplomat, although underneath his smile he was busy with the strategy of a general.

This strategy included a steady stream of correspondence to Giraud. De Gaulle declared that both the Algerians and the Free French wanted him to be the

Charles de Gaulle at a press conference in Algiers in 1944.

military leader in Algeria. Furthermore, they disapproved of Giraud's support of Vichy France. He pointed out that Free French supporters in France were painting the cross of Lorraine on walls, barns, and sidewalks. "All France is with me," he said. "France is Gaullist, fiercely Gaullist." Finally Giraud accepted a proposal which named de Gaulle as head of France's wartime provisional government, with Algiers as the capital.

As he left London for Algiers in May 1943, de Gaulle showed his affection for Churchill by joking, "I believe I have discovered the reason for our misunderstandings...I have noticed that you are always in a bad temper when you are wrong. On the other hand, I am always in a bad temper when I am right but can't convince you of it. So when we meet, both of us are always in a bad temper." The two men laughed.

The de Gaulle family moved into a villa surrounded by olive trees just south of Algiers. Yvonne made one public appearance there when she went to Gibraltar for a formal welcome by the governor. Then she dropped out of public view while she spent her time caring for Charles and Anne and knitting clothes for the babies of the officers and men of the Free French forces.

The de Gaulles ordered a movie projector, a screen, and a copy of Walt Disney's *Snow White and the Seven Dwarfs*, a movie Anne never tired of watching. Elisabeth left her studies at Oxford to work in a press office of the French Committee in Algiers. Philippe continued his duties with the Free French Navy in the North Atlantic Ocean and the English Channel.

By the end of 1943, hundreds of Gaullists had left occupied France to rally around their leader in Algiers. Soldiers, career diplomats, civil servants, bankers, and labor leaders crossed the sea to join the forces that they believed would liberate their country.

De Gaulle also found growing support in London among leaders of countries that had been invaded by Germany. Like de Gaulle, these leaders were attempting to maintain a political force that would be ready to take over when the Germans surrendered. They responded to de Gaulle's personal appeals. In two weeks, he convinced leaders of Czechoslovakia, Poland, Belgium, Luxembourg, Yugoslavia, and Norway to recognize his Provisional Government as the legal authority in France.

For de Gaulle, the growth of Free France justified his increasing demands for equality with Allied leaders. For the Allies, his demands created problems and conflicts. President Roosevelt wanted to ignore de Gaulle. Churchill was less hostile, but he did not want to offend his long-standing ally, Roosevelt. Premier Stalin of Russia was willing to accept de Gaulle as leader but did not wish to offend the other Allies.

Plans were made for the long-awaited Allied invasion of France. The Allies scheduled a joint broadcast over BBC radio in which allied heads of state would announce the invasion to their people. De Gaulle was scheduled to speak after the king of Norway, the queen of the Netherlands, the grand duchess of Luxembourg, the prime minister of Belgium, and American General Dwight D. Eisenhower, who was the Supreme Commander of Allied Forces. De Gaulle refused to be the last speaker. He also insisted on writing his own speech—one in which he ordered French citizens to obey his orders from that time on.

On June 5, 1944, twenty-three thousand airborne

troops and over a quarter of a million British, Canadian, and American soldiers invaded the beaches of northern France. This attack forced the Germans to retreat from their fortified positions along the Atlantic coast and to regroup inland. It would be only a matter of time before France was liberated. The day later became known as D day.

De Gaulle was confident of victory, yet sympathetic to the cost. He wrote: "Fighting France has assuredly grown solid and coherent. But how many losses, sorrows, agonies have been required to pay for this result?"

About a week later, de Gaulle boarded the destroyer *La Combattante*, heading across the English Channel toward France. For four hours he stood on the deck in the chilly wind, scanning the horizon through binoculars, straining for the first glimpse of his beloved country. Five years before, he had left in defeat with only a dream to sustain him. Now he returned to make that dream come true.

He had planned his political strategy as carefully as he had always planned his military strategy. On the ship with him were ten men who had proven their loyalty to him. In France, leaders were ready and waiting for his orders. He had a list of de Gaulle supporters to use in selecting police chiefs, mayors, teachers, and others whose support would be vital to his government.

De Gaulle lands on French soil in Normandy on June 14, 1944.

De Gaulle traveled to three different towns, using the same strategy in each. First, he sent a car cruising over the streets, announcing through a loudspeaker that General de Gaulle, the liberator of France, was coming to talk to his people. Next came a group of gendarmes, French policemen, who helped the citizens decorate the town square with flowers and banners.

Then de Gaulle himself arrived in his hip-length military jacket with shining stars on the sleeve and his gold-braided cap. He made his way through the crowds, shaking hands. After a high mass at the cathedral, he mounted a platform backed by four flags—the French, the British, the American, and the cross of Lorraine. He spoke briefly, saying, "I promise you that we shall continue to fight until sovereignty is reestablished over every inch of our soil." Then he led the crowd in the singing of the "Marseillaise."

Chapter / Six

I Am President of the Republic

De Gaulle faced competition for power on all sides. First, there were the Germans, who had not yet surrendered. Then there were the Resistance leaders, who had already proven their leadership, courage, and patriotism. Also, some political party leaders, especially Communists, were eager to step in when the Germans left. A fourth group was the collaborators, who already had control of many government offices. Finally, the Allies, especially the Americans, did not support him.

At that moment, French citizens were more interested in a liberator than in a political leader. So de Gaulle planned to be in Paris to march down the streets as their liberator.

However, he could not arrive in the capital before the Germans had surrendered control of the city. He had waited impatiently in Alergia while the Allies pushed closer to Paris. His spies in Paris told him that Resistance fighters now dared to attack German soldiers who ventured out alone. Some citizens were shaking the dust from French flags that had been hidden away for four years.

On August 16, de Gaulle ordered the Allied Command to send a plane to fly him to France. He was suspicious when officials said the plane needed repairs because it had overshot the runway when it arrived. A replacement plane arrived. This one needed repairs for a tire that burst. De Gaulle announced, "I shall leave at eleven o'clock as scheduled, and I shall leave in my own plane." He left in a French plane and arrived in Cherbourg the next day.

The liberation of Paris began without him. Resistance fighters in the capital fired openly on the Germans while de Gaulle was still in Cherbourg. As soon as he heard this, de Gaulle informed Allied Supreme Commander Dwight Eisenhower that he and French General Jacques LeClerc were heading for Paris and that they needed Allied military support. Eisenhower agreed. Just after midnight on August 22, Adolf Hitler ordered German officers in Paris to destroy the city.

The officers destroyed a telephone center. General Dietrich von Choltitz, German commander of Paris, ordered his men to place a ton of explosives in the

De Gaulle arrives in Cherbourg on August 17, 1944.

Chamber of Deputies, the meeting place of the National Assembly, and three more tons in Notre Dame Cathedral. Then he hesitated, unable to bring himself to give the order to destroy these beautiful buildings. When Hitler repeated the order, von Choltitz answered that too many Germans would be needlessly killed in an explosion. Thus both the buildings and many French and German lives were spared.

Just before three o'clock on the afternoon of August 25, Philippe de Gaulle, son of Charles, rode into Paris in a tank. He was an ensign in the First

Regiment of Marines, and he had captured a German major, who sat at his side.

Shortly after that, Charles de Gaulle rode through the suburbs in a small motorcade of three black sedans and two jeeps mounted with machine guns. Hundreds of French tanks roared through the outskirts, headed for the center of the city. Church bells rang, and the "Marseillaise" blared from loudspeakers. French soldiers marched down the city streets, their way almost blocked by cheering, laughing, crying Parisians. Most of the Nazis were hiding from the liberators.

Lieutenant Henri Karcher was the first French soldier to reach the Maurice Hotel, where von Choltitz had his office. He rushed up the stairs to the second floor and burst in on von Choltitz.

Von Choltitz stood.

Karcher saluted. "Lieutenant Henri Karcher of the Army of General de Gaulle," he announced.

"General von Choltitz, commander of Gross Paris," was the answer.

"Are you ready to surrender?"

"Yes," answered von Choltitz.

"Then you are my prisoner," said Karcher.

That afternoon, citizens lined the streets as von Choltitz, in a closely guarded armored car, was taken to sign the surrender papers. Georges Bidault, president of the National Resistance Council, waited impatiently

General de Gaulle reads the surrender papers signed by von Choltitz.

for de Gaulle. He had planned that he and de Gaulle would appear for the crowds together.

De Gaulle kept him waiting while he made two moves to emphasize his role as a political leader. First, he examined the surrender papers. Then he shook hands all around at the police station, thanking the men for their cooperation during the liberation and enlisting their support for the days to come.

Finally he met with Bidault. Bidault told him of his

plan to announce to the crowds that a new republic was about to begin.

"No," answered de Gaulle. "The Republic has never ceased to exist. I am President of the Republic."

De Gaulle stepped to the balcony that looked over the Seine. From sidewalk to sidewalk, every inch of the broad boulevard was crammed with people. Above the street, people crowded onto rooftops and clung to lampposts and flagpoles. Perhaps as many as two million people chanted, "De Gaulle, de Gaulle, de Gaulle." For a few minutes, he waved and smiled at the crowds. Then he turned back into the building. He had important work to do.

Allied and French military leaders reacted quickly when de Gaulle began to issue orders for his victory march through the streets of Paris the next day. They pointed out that this would be extremely dangerous. German regiments were still pressing toward Paris, ninety German bombers were at the Paris airport, and German soldiers were everywhere. De Gaulle refused to listen. "Since each of those here has chosen Charles de Gaulle in his heart...I must allow the man to be seen."

The next afternoon, de Gaulle led the parade. First, he placed a wreath in the shape of the cross of Lorraine on the Tomb of the Unknown Soldier. Then he walked down the broad Champs-Elysées behind four French tanks. Members of his Provisional

Government marched directly behind him. Behind them were Resistance leaders and masses of cheering citizens shouting, "Long live France! Long live de Gaulle! Long live peace!" Soon the marchers could see the famous gargoyles of Notre Dame Cathedral, where de Gaulle was to worship in the first mass of the liberation.

Suddenly shots rang out. De Gaulle proceeded calmly into the cathedral. He seemed not to notice that a few more shots were fired in the church. None of them hit him. After the ceremony, he marched back into the streets and continued his walk, as though there were no danger.

De Gaulle had escaped the would-be killers, but many French were not so lucky. The Germans were still in control in many areas of France. They sent hundreds of French prisoners to labor camps in Germany. In some villages, they massacred the inhabitants and set fire to buildings. They tortured imprisoned Resistance members.

The Germans were not the only threat to a return to peaceful living. French citizens scoured the countryside looking for the collaborators who had helped the Nazis. Some collaborators were put on trial; others were simply shot on sight.

De Gaulle criticized those who sought revenge. "In spite of everything, no individual has the right to punish the guilty; it is the State's concern." Still the killing continued. Perhaps as many as forty thousand known and suspected collaborators were killed in France in the year after the war.

In September, Madame de Gaulle and Anne moved from Algiers to a comfortable home near Paris. Yvonne de Gaulle said about the new house that it was "rather better than what I wanted."

De Gaulle now traveled through the liberated areas of France, declaring himself the ruler of the country. In the six-week tour, about ten million citizens turned out to wave flags and cheer, "Long live de Gaulle!" In each town, he appointed mayors, judges, chiefs of police, and newspaper editors.

The United States, Britain, and the Soviet Union recognized the Provisional Government as the ruling power in France. But Eisenhower refused when de Gaulle asked for supplies and equipment for French soldiers. Churchill also refused. They did not want to involve the French forces in the last battles of the war.

Then Churchill made a request of de Gaulle, and it was de Gaulle's turn to refuse. Churchill asked him to sign a pact of mutual defense between England and France. De Gaulle answered that he could not trust Britain to be faithful to that pact. De Gaulle traveled to Moscow because he thought he could gain support from French Communists if he had the support of the

Russian Communist premier, Joseph Stalin. Premier Stalin agreed, on the condition that de Gaulle would support Russian control over Poland. De Gaulle refused.

Stalin agreed to omit the condition. But at the signing ceremony, de Gaulle discovered that the condition remained. He was furious. "France has been insulted," he said, and he turned to leave. Immediately, Stalin handed him the new pact. Both men signed it.

Later de Gaulle wrote in his memoirs that Stalin had congratulated him, saying, "You played your hand well."

De Gaulle showed the same determination in his insistence that French soldiers play an important part in the war. Once, when General Eisenhower ordered the Allies to retreat from Strasbourg, a French city on the German border, de Gaulle ordered French troops not to follow those orders. Another time, de Gaulle ordered French troops to join Allied forces in Germany "even if the Americans do not agree and if you should have to cross it [the Rhine] in rowing boats." He also moved French troops into northern Italy without Allied approval. The United States threatened to cut off supplies to French soldiers. De Gaulle was able to negotiate a compromise to allow a token force of French soldiers to remain.

In February, Roosevelt, Churchill, and Stalin met in Yalta, in southern Ukraine, to discuss plans for the peace which they knew would come soon. Churchill explained why they did not invite de Gaulle. "I cannot think of anything more unpleasant and impossible than having this menacing and hostile man in your midst, always trying to make himself a reputation in France...."

At that meeting, the leaders made plans to divide Germany into occupied zones after the war. Stalin declared that only the Soviet Union, the United States, and Britain had earned the right to occupy a zone. Roosevelt argued that France should be given a zone as an act of kindness. Churchill wanted France included because he worried that Britain might need France as an ally at some time. When Stalin refused, the United States and Britain each gave up some of their territory to create a fourth zone.

They also made plans to establish the United Nations, an organization devoted to world peace. De Gaulle refused to join, since he had not been included in the planning sessions.

Finally the war ended. In May 1945, Germany signed the surrender papers. On August 6, the United States dropped the first atomic bomb on Japan, and on August 14, the Japanese surrendered.

De Gaulle could now turn his attention to his own country. The situation in France was grave. Whole towns and cities were in ruins. Food, clothing, and

De Gaulle in Paris on V-E Day, May 8, 1945.

shelter were scarce. Many factories had been converted to making war supplies and could not easily be retooled. Germans had destroyed railroad cars, trucks, buses, and automobiles. Homes and other buildings had been destroyed, and no materials were available for rebuilding. Perhaps most critical was the lack of manpower. About a million and a half workers had been lost because of the war.

In private, de Gaulle remarked, "War is horrible, but as for peace, it is exasperating."

Chapter / Seven

Good-bye, Gentlemen

De Gaulle was unanimously elected the premier of France by the French National Assembly just before his fifty-fifth birthday. However, he had little power because he lacked the support of National Assembly representatives.

He used a special presidential privilege to save Pétain's life. His former best friend and instructor was sentenced to death as a traitor. De Gaulle changed the sentence to life imprisonment.

De Gaulle appealed to the citizens to work together, but he did not trust them to do so. He feared that businessmen, farmers, and factory owners would take advantage of a public that was eager to make up for four years of deprivation suffered under the occupation. He established regulations for prices, wages, and working conditions, and he put mines, automobile factories, banks, and gas and electric companies under government control.

The result was the opposite of what he had expected. Farmers and factory owners set up "black markets" where they sold their goods for prices much higher than allowed by law. Mines and electric companies did not produce adequate fuel for the nation. Their managers blamed this on government regulations. Workers went on strike, creating water and electric shortages, transportation delays, and shortages of food and supplies.

De Gaulle's solution was to tighten regulations, although he knew the National Assembly would not support this. The struggle between de Gaulle and the National Assembly ended in a surprise move by the president.

In January 1946, he sent motorcycle policemen to the homes of each cabinet minister, requesting that they appear at a cabinet meeting on the next day. He gave no explanation for the summons. The seventeen anxious members arrived at de Gaulle's office as requested.

Promptly at noon, the president, in full military uniform, joined them. They stood as he entered. He shook hands all around, but he did not invite them to be seated. His message was brief: "The exclusive regime of the parties has come back...I disapprove of it...I must therefore retire."

He nodded a farewell. When the ministers tried to question him, he cut them short. "My decision is not subject to discussion. Good-bye, gentlemen."

Perhaps de Gaulle had hoped to be called back by popular vote. If so, he was disappointed. His colleagues did not contact him. The press ignored him. A poll taken shortly after he stepped down indicated that most citizens were not sorry to see him go. Perhaps he had created too much conflict. Perhaps his arrogance had made him too unapproachable. Perhaps citizens were simply more interested in their private and business lives than they were in national leadership.

However, he drew cheering crowds as he traveled as a private citizen throughout France and its territories in the next six months. François Mauriac, a Nobel-prize-winning novelist, explained de Gaulle's appeal: "[he]...has made us believe that she [France] is that great nation still....There are still millions of Frenchmen who have not forgotten him." De Gaulle's fans were cheering for their liberator, not for the political leader of France. There was no movement to persuade him to enter government service again.

Charles and Yvonne settled down in Colombey, a town of 365 people. One of Yvonne's projects was to plant a flower bed shaped like the cross of Lorraine.

Charles spent his time reading and working on his memoirs. He began his autobiography with the statement: "I have always had a certain idea about France." He also enjoyed taking walks on his property. "I have walked around our little property fifteen thousand times," he bragged. "In the tumult of men and events, solitude was my temptation; now it is my friend." They had few guests except their children Philippe and Elisabeth and their families. Philippe's son, Charles de Gaulle, was a special joy to his grandfather. Philippe continued his career in the navy, and Elisabeth was the wife of a young army officer.

The de Gaulles had little money. Some dinner guests even complained that they had gone away hungry. Menus included such simple food as pigs' feet, cabbage, and tripe. At one dinner, Charles asked Yvonne, "My dear, don't we have something better for our friends?" She answered simply, "No." More often than not, water was served instead of wine. They no longer had a chauffeur, and Madame de Gaulle had to learn to drive. Yvonne seemed to prefer this life. "My ideal wardrobe," she said, "is two black dresses; one on my back and one in the wash."

General and Madame de Gaulle had long worried about what would happen to their daughter Anne when they were no longer around to care for her. They agreed that all the royalties from Charles' books would

Cheering crowds welcomed de Gaulle when he toured France as a private citizen.

go to the Anne de Gaulle Foundation, an organization to help handicapped children. They also made arrangements to establish a small home, staffed by nuns who could care for Anne and others like her. Unfortunately, Anne died of pneumonia just two years later, at the age of twenty. At her graveside, de Gaulle shed tears and said prayers. Then he spoke about his child, who had always been different from other children. "Now she is like the others."

The man who had once ruled France seemed content with his family, his writing, and his books. Still, he criticized government leaders for not solving major problems—an inflation rate of fifty percent, rebellion in the French Indo-China colonies, and conflict among National Assembly members. Saying "I shall remain the nation's guide," he reminded audiences that he had not left government for good.

Finally, he felt he could no longer remain a private citizen. In April 1947, he reentered politics dramatically. In Strasbourg, he stood on a platform draped in the blue, white and red banners of France. He raised his long arms in the V sign for victory. "I am calling on all Frenchmen to join me in a new adventure. Today is the birth of the *Rassemblement Populaire Français* [Rally of the French People]...." He promised to bring prosperity to France and to make the country great again. In just two weeks, eight hundred thousand citizens signed petitions, attended meetings, and announced their interest in the new RPF party.

De Gaulle called them to dreams of a glorious country. For a while they forgot high prices, food shortages, and low wages. In the October 1947 municipal elections, the RPF party polled more than forty percent of the votes.

Prosperity did come to France, but before de Gaulle and the RPF could claim credit. American ships brought in tons of grain and flour as part of a project called the Marshall Plan. This U.S. aid program was designed to help rebuild war-torn Europe. Spring crops were excellent, and produce appeared in markets all over the country. Tourists once again visited France, giving a boost to hotels, restaurants, and industry. French citizens no longer needed a promise of prosperity, and membership in the RPF declined.

De Gaulle lost interest in the party. In 1951, he said sadly, "I had thought to rally the French people... I have failed to bring it off."

Again he returned to writing, determined to finish his three-volume series, *Mémoires de Guerre (Memories of War)*. He spent hours in the tower room at Colombey, which he had designed in the shape of a hexagon to symbolize the shape of France. His daughter Elisabeth, one of the few people who could read her father's handwriting, typed for him.

From the sidelines, de Gaulle watched the growing turmoil in Algeria. The struggle for independence was not unexpected. In 1830, France had invaded and conquered Algeria. From that time, Algeria was under French rule. About a million French and other European businessmen, called *colons*, prospered there, making a profit from the fertile fields of wheat, barley, grapes, and olives and from the manufacture of construction materials. About eight million Algerian Arabs were excluded from these ventures. The colons were quick to block reforms which would give the Arabs an equal voice in politics and the economy.

During World War II, Algeria was ruled first by the Vichy government and then by the Allies. Arabs resented these leaders, who were imposed on them. After the war, they began to call for independence from France. French leaders rejected this suggestion. When the rebels began to demonstrate, the French government sent military police to quiet them.

The situation grew tense. Arab leaders carried out ambushes, assassinations, and bombing raids against the French military forces in Algeria. The troops responded by destroying native croplands and orchards and forcing millions of Arabs into concentration camps.

Many of the colons and tens of thousands of Arabs had strong personal, family, and business ties with France. They fled to the mother country to escape the

General de Gaulle lights the flame at the Tomb of the Unknown Soldier in Paris in 1948.

De Gaulle tours North Africa in 1957.

killing and destruction. There the refugees joined others who demanded that the government stop the bloodshed. They responded to de Gaulle when he offered to help: "It may be that I would intervene again." But French government officials did not respond to him. He refused to enter the conflict except as an official representative of the French government.

Leon Delbecque, a former RPF member, went to Algiers in early 1958 to organize de Gaulle supporters there in a group called the Committee of Vigilance. Then he returned to France to tell de Gaulle, "There is only one man who can save the Republic—de Gaulle. Will you reply Yes?"

De Gaulle answered, "Delbecque, I have always had a habit of accepting my responsibilities."

But de Gaulle could not nominate himself to office, and French President Coty ignored him.

Leaders of both movements incited the crowds to riot. In Algiers, a million angry people streamed into government offices. They overturned desks and other furniture and threw books and records out the windows. The demonstrations spread to France, where Arabs and their supporters crowded into the broad Champs-Elysées, shouting against French leaders, "Throw them into the Seine!" Thousands fought in the streets with clubs and fists. Policemen rushed in, some to try to stop the demonstrators, others to help them.

In Algiers on May 15, Delbecque and his newly organized Committee of Vigilance led a demonstration demanding French control of the country. Claiming to have the backing of French generals in Algeria, Delbecque issued an ultimatum to President Coty: Either install General de Gaulle immediately as French premier, he demanded, or we will take over, first in Algeria and then in France itself.

De Gaulle called a press conference. Still tall and

Charles de Gaulle in 1958.

straight-shouldered, he wore a gray double-breasted suit and a pearl-gray necktie. He showed his age by the graying hair and deep circles under his eyes, but he was as ready mentally and emotionally as he had been when the High Command had first given him permission to advance against the Germans in 1940. He announced: "Once before, the country in the depths of its being, gave me the trust to lead it...Today it should know that I hold myself ready to take over the powers of the Republic."

Then he arranged to talk with Premier Pflimlin in a park in a Paris suburb at 11:30 that night. At that secret meeting, Pflimlin offered to resign so that de Gaulle could become premier. However, Pflimlin imposed two conditions. The first was that de Gaulle speak against the Algerian rebels. De Gaulle answered, "No, I will not condemn." The second condition was that de Gaulle cooperate with French and Algerian leaders. Again de Gaulle refused, saying, "I stand above the conflict, and I must have power unhampered by the parties and their conditions." At 1:30 the next morning, the meeting ended with no agreement.

A few days later, Pflimlin resigned. President Coty announced, "I have called on the most illustrious of Frenchmen...to establish the Republic."

Chapter/ Eight

Those Gentlemen Are Poor Shots

On June 1, de Gaulle was voted premier by the National Assembly, winning by 329 to 224 votes. Immediately he made two demands. First, he requested full emergency powers for six months. Second, he requested that a new constitution be offered to the citizens by public referendum as soon as possible. Both demands were granted.

Without taking sides for either independence or French control, he flew to Algiers, where he stood in an open car, waving to the crowds that greeted him. The police could hardly control his supporters—Moslem men in knee-length cloaks, woman in long, loose dresses and veils, children waving French flags and selling miniature crosses of Lorraine. They lined the streets and sidewalks, crowded onto porches and hung out of windows, waving and chanting, "Algerie Française" ["Algeria wants to be part of France"]. The rebels also waved their banners and shouted their slogans. De Gaulle finally signaled them to be quiet. Slowly and dramatically, he said, "I have understood you." The crowds resumed their cheering.

After de Gaulle returned to France, the people in Algeria asked: "What did he mean?" "What did he understand about us?" "What will happen now?" They realized that they had cheered for the man, not for his message. Officials contacted de Gaulle's aides for an explanation. They received no answer. In a few days, the country was again torn by demonstrations and riots.

Probably de Gaulle himself was undecided. If he supported independence, France would lose a valuable colony and, perhaps, some prestige in the eyes of the world. If he supported French control, the rebels would step up their violence, feeling that they had lost every- thing, anyway. In this matter as in all others, de Gaulle first asked himself: What will be best for France? The answer was not clear to him at that time.

Charles de Gaulle would return to the Algerian problem once he had the authority he needed. Determined that he would never again be frustrated by a National Assembly which rejected his ideas, he selected a team to write a new constitution. He told them to restrict the power of the National Assembly, giving the president the last word. He also insisted that the president have the right to submit measures directly to the public in a referendum. He regretted that no constitutional change could alter the party system in France. There are too many parties, he said: "They make me want to vomit." When asked what party he represented, de Gaulle answered, "De Gaulle is above parties."

He campaigned for the constitution throughout the country, with Yvonne at his side.

In September 1958, twenty years after he first criticized the old constitution, de Gaulle submitted the new constitution to citizens in a public referendum. He made a personal appeal: "To each and every one of you, I entrust the fate of France." The referendum was approved by eighty percent of the population.

The constitution now reflected his views on presidential power, but Charles de Gaulle was premier, not president. President Coty still had two more years in office. Aware of de Gaulle's popularity, Coty said that he would not oppose de Gaulle in an election.

De Gaulle easily won the office in December 1958, capturing seventy-eight percent of the vote. When he addressed the National Assembly, he spoke confidently about his plans. The representatives could no longer restrict his power as they had before.

The ceremony of the transfer of presidential powers to General de Gaulle on January 8, 1959.

The new president remembered the awe he had felt at his first glimpse of the Saint-Cyr officers' uniform. He ordered that all personnel, from footmen to officers, wear dress uniforms of dark blue and red, white gloves, and plume helmets at his new home and offices, the Elysée Palace.

De Gaulle immediately organized a strict schedule for himself. He had a brief breakfast with Madame de Gaulle at 7:30, and then he spent about an hour studying French and foreign news reports. After meeting with his personal staff, he often received visitors for two

President and Madame de Gaulle's new home in 1959–the Elysée Palace.

or three hours. After lunch, he worked on official papers for five or more hours.

President and Madame de Gaulle shared quiet dinners and evenings together whenever possible. They preferred to spend time at Colombey, where they enjoyed more privacy. A niece said that living at the palace was "...a real privation for Aunt Yvonne...she is a very good housekeeper and likes to oversee her kitchen...but like a good soldier's wife, she had adapted herself."

They invited the public to join them at the palace on holidays, like Mother's Day and Christmas. On other special occasions, they and other government officials welcomed guests for questioning and photographs. The de Gaulles were gracious hosts.

The Algerian situation continued to drain France of money, supplies, and personnel. De Gaulle tried in vain to convince the rebels to negotiate a settlement.

In Paris, demonstrators hid bombs in cars and threw them into apartments, restaurants, and shopping centers. Frequently, police were called in to break up street fights.

De Gaulle answered, "That's absurd" when aides suggested that he have bodyguards. They insisted and he finally agreed, but he warned, "Keep them out of my sight." Officials increased the number of sentries around the Elysée Palace, and a bodyguard slept in a corridor outside the de Gaulles' bedroom.

Unable to make progress in negotiating a settlement, de Gaulle used the right of presidential referendum that he had gained under the new constitution. In January 1961, citizens in both France and Algeria were asked: Should the Algerians be allowed to vote on whether they want independence? In France, seventy-six percent of the people voted yes, and in Algeria, seventy percent voted yes.

Soon afterward in Algeria, a group of French

officers took matters into their own hands. General Maurice Challe, the French commander in chief, took control of the main public buildings in Algiers. He imprisoned the Gaullist leader, General Gambiez. On April 21, 1961, Challe broadcast the news that he and his fellow officers controlled the country. A few moments after that broadcast, President de Gaulle was stopped in the lobby of a theater, where he had just seen a play. An aide handed him a short message: The French rebels have taken over Algeria.

De Gaulle made a quick decision. There was no time to send troops or to attempt negotiations. He had only the power of his personality and the authority of his office—and the magic of television. Within a few hours, he was ready. Millions of viewers in France and Algeria sat in front of their television sets and saw their president in full general's uniform, with the cross of Lorraine on his chest. They listened as he urged true patriots to fight back against the rebel French leaders. First he made his personal appeal to the citizens: "Frenchmen, Frenchwomen! Help me!" He continued: "I forbid every Frenchman, and above all every soldier, to carry out the orders of any of these generals."

His plea worked. Within three days, the rebel generals were without support. De Gaulle had saved Algeria from a takeover by rebel officers in the French military.

Despite this victory, de Gaulle had not won the battle. The conflict continued. Countless persons were victims of false imprisonment, beating, torture, and killings. In seven years of fighting, the French lost fifteen thousand men, and the Algerians one hundred fifty thousand.

De Gaulle himself was not safe from the violence. In September 1961, assassins waited as he drove from Paris to his home in Colombey. Under a pile of sand beside the road, they had hidden a cylinder containing ninety pounds of explosives and some butane gas, along with a gas can containing petrol, oil, and soap flakes. As the President's car passed the targeted spot, a sheet of flame suddenly enveloped it. Fortunately, the cylinder failed to explode, and the chauffeur was able to speed through the flames.

On another occasion, de Gaulle's car was ambushed by gunmen hiding along the sides of the road. Twelve bullets hit the car and blew out the tires on the right side. The chauffeur accelerated to ninety miles an hour and somehow was able to keep the car on the road. With the same calmness that he had shown at Notre Dame Cathedral in 1944, de Gaulle remarked, "This is getting to be dangerous. Fortunately, these gentlemen are poor shots."

Finally, in March of 1962, de Gaulle persuaded both sides to agree on a cease-fire and on a one-question referendum: Should Algeria be granted independence?

In that referendum, over 90 percent of the eligible voters cast a ballot. Ninety-nine percent voted for independence.

On July 3, 1962, an independent Algeria was born. All over the country, French flags were taken down. The new Algerian flags, green and white stripes with a red crescent and a star, were raised.

Chapter / Nine

The Alternative to de Gaulle Is Chaos

Now de Gaulle could turn his attention to other matters, and he did not like what he saw. For one thing, France's longtime enemy, Germany, was rapidly increasing its economic and political power. Also, a new spirit of international cooperation for defense, trade, science, and culture was spreading throughout Europe. De Gaulle did not want to be part of this. "To cooperate is to lose one's independence," he said. Besides, he still resented the Allied leaders who had excluded him from decision making during World War II.

The former Allies had created the North Atlantic Treaty Organization (NATO) as a mutual defense against possible attacks. De Gaulle had allowed NATO to maintain bases in France, but he was not an

General de Gaulle among the crowd in Strasbourg on November 23, 1963.

enthusiastic supporter. Increasingly, he felt that NATO regulations and projects were encroaching on his independence. In March 1965, without even notifying his cabinet, he announced that France was withdrawing from NATO. He demanded that all NATO personnel and installations be removed from French territory by April 1967.

De Gaulle was confident of reelection as his seven-year term as president drew to a close. Because he believed that he was fulfilling his promise to rebuild France, he remained aloof from the campaign.

His five opponents waged an all-out attack. They reminded voters that de Gaulle had not allowed France to participate in international programs, and that he had been unable to prevent strikes by miners, transportation workers, and milk producers.

In the balloting in December 1965, de Gaulle received only 44 percent of the vote. The runner-up was François Mitterrand, who headed a joint Communist/Socialist ticket.

A rumor spread that de Gaulle was so disgusted with the French voters that at first he refused to submit to a runoff election. But Charles de Gaulle did not admit defeat. He adopted the slogan, "The alternative to de Gaulle is chaos." Then he directed a dramatic campaign that resulted in a victory for him with 54 percent of the vote.

In that campaign, as in all her husband's activities, Yvonne de Gaulle remained quietly loyal. According to a family friend, "Few people realize how much the General depends on Yvonne. She has sustained him all these years."

Madame de Gaulle was a small, rather plain woman, and so inconspicuous that she was able to walk unnoticed on the streets of Paris. However, she did not hesitate to stand up for her strong Roman Catholic beliefs. She never invited a divorced person to her home. Once she persuaded Charles not to appoint an otherwise qualified man to the Cabinet because he had been divorced. She also spoke in favor of laws banning books and movies that she considered morally offensive.

Although her only interest in politics was to serve her husband, Madame de Gaulle was a gracious hostess at many state banquets for dignitaries from all over the world. The French people felt affection for her and, because of her modest ways, they sometimes called her Aunt Yvonne.

By contrast, they referred to her husband as King Charles. Perhaps he was thinking of creating a monument to himself when King Charles made plans to modernize Paris. He began with Les Halles, an open-air market covering many square blocks on the right bank of the Seine. For a century and a half, shoppers had come there to buy fresh turnips, potatoes, apples, fish, and meat. They sipped on fresh onion soup and chewed on freshly baked bread while they chatted with friends. The tradition was strong, but the buildings and equipment were shabby and worn. Previous French rulers had wanted to renovate this market, but none had been able to acquire the necessary money and public support.

De Gaulle was able to carry out the plans. Throughout his political career, he had referred to the greatness of France. Citizens accepted the modernization as one more symbol of this greatness. Under de Gaulle, a new efficient market was built, complete with refrigerated warehouses and railroad and trucking facilities. He also supervised the building of wide boulevards, high-rise apartments, and a subway which was considered the finest public transportation network in the world. The president even ordered that the famous buildings of Paris be scrubbed and cleaned.

He also kept contact with the less sophisticated areas of the country. De Gaulle was warm and friendly in his visits to his people. He toured Paris suburb by suburb. Throughout the country, he shook hands with tens of thousands of voters, conferred with local officials, and patted little children on the head. In the grape-growing areas of Languedoc, he talked about wine. In the manufacturing city of Lyons, he talked about textiles. He knew the needs of each small village, and he brought hope that residents would soon have a better water supply, a more efficient communications system, or a new highway.

Listeners sometimes accused him of memorizing his speeches because he spoke so eloquently. This was not true. He was eloquent because he spent about two hours every day writing, crossing out, and rewriting his speeches. Since he worked so long on each sentence, he could easily recall the words when he was in front of the crowds. He did, however, hire an actor to coach him in dictation and gestures.

De Gaulle had strong support and strong opposition. His supporters pointed to the fact that France had become a powerful competitor against neighboring Belgium, West Germany, the United Kingdom, and the Netherlands. His opponents criticized his refusal to accept criticisms and suggestions. They also opposed his insistence on a balanced budget and strong government control of business.

Workers were angered by his belief that wages must be kept low in order to keep prices down. In January 1969, thousand of workers demonstrated at a large Renault factory. Shipping workers and aviation workers immediately joined the auto workers in protest. When coal miners went on strike, de Gaulle threatened to draft them into the armed forces. This angered workers all over the country.

Soon nine million workers were involved. Transportation workers went on strike, and people could not get to work. People were without heat and light when the gas and electric workers also decided to go on strike. Food stores closed when truckers and wholesalers refused to work. Reporters and typesetters stopped working, and there were no newspapers. Piles of garbage rotted on the streets when the sanitation workers joined the other strikers.

Political demonstrators added to the upheaval. These included Communists and anti-Communists, opponents and supporters of the Vietnam War, and thousands of others.

Students joined the demonstrations. They compared their schools to de Gaulle, calling them old-fashioned, inadequate, and accessible only to the rich. Rioters dragged piles of paper, furniture, and rags into the streets and set fire to them.

His aides begged de Gaulle to quiet the violence by freeing arrested students and calling off the police. He answered, "No, no, and again no! The State does not back down."

On May 13, de Gaulle's seventy-eighth birthday, hundreds of thousands of strikers, students, and other demonstrators marched and shouted and waved banners saying "De Gaulle to the museum!" and "Enough of de Gaulle!"

He had just one more weapon—his TV magic. On May 24, he appeared on television to announce that he had a solution to the conflict. He first reminded the audience, "For 30 years, I have led France to its destiny, and I am ready to do it again." Then he described his solution. First, he would ban all protests immediately. Then he would schedule a public referendum by which citizens could express their views peacefully by voting. He gave no more details. He ended by asking demonstrators to stop rioting so he could get on with the business of governing.

This time the de Gaulle magic did not work. Within hours of the broadcast, protestors were demonstrating with the same violence as before.

De Gaulle had tried and lost. He remained alone in the Elysée Palace, wondering why the French people had not responded this time. He was angry, telling himself, "The French are cattle. Just cattle."

Outside the Elysée, leaders and citizens shouted for his resignation. All over France, journalists and editors, politicians and military men, workers and students were asking one question: Would the man who had spent his life working for France resign now when his country was on the verge of civil war?

At 9:15 on the morning of May 29, de Gaulle cancelled the weekly meeting of the Council of Ministers. His secretary told them, "The general asks me to inform you that he is going to Colombey for twenty-four hours. The council meeting is deferred until tomorrow at 3:00 P.M." Headlines in French newspapers and all over the world predicted that de Gaulle would resign.

By noon the next day, the de Gaulles had not appeared at Colombey. At 2:00 P.M., Secretary-General Bernard Tricot announced, "The general has disappeared." Two hours later, the minister of the armed forces had a single statement for the press: "The President has flown to Germany."

De Gaulle himself sent out the next bulletin. He

announced that he would explain his next moves at 4:30 on the afternoon of May 30. Since the national TV system had been put out of order by rioting, he would make a radio broadcast.

Millions of private citizens and hundreds of political leaders gathered around their radios, most of them expecting to hear the president resign. They did not know that de Gaulle had convinced the president that France needed him, and that he must not resign.

De Gaulle's voice was strong, and his words were dramatic: "In present circumstances, I shall not retire. I have a mandate from the people. I shall fulfill it...No! The Republic shall not abdicate." He spoke for less than five minutes. He said he would dissolve the Assembly and organize citizen groups to stop the conflict. If these moves did not succeed, he was ready to "adopt other methods." The meaning was clear. He was prepared to announce a national emergency, if necessary. This would allow him to take control of the police and the armed forces. Far from retiring, de Gaulle was determined and eager to serve his country.

This time the old de Gaulle magic worked. Groups of government leaders began to sing the "Marseillaise." About a million citizens gathered in the middle of Paris, crowding the Champs-Elysées from sidewalk to sidewalk, dancing and cheering for their leader and his promises.

The very next day, cars, trucks, and buses traveled

peacefully down the streets of Paris. On the first Monday after the speech, thousands of workers returned to their factories. By the end of that week, almost all strikes were over. Slowly at first, but surely, the demonstrators quieted. Students went back to campuses, fearful that they might not receive their all-important diplomas. Police work nearly returned to normal.

In the June 30 elections, de Gaulle's party, now called the *Union pour la Nouvelle Republique*, or UNR, received a clear majority of the votes. Once again, de Gaulle took control. He fired Prime Minister Pompidou. He also fired sixty radio and TV journalists who had spoken and written against him. He sent police to universities and factories to round up strike leaders.

He had control, but he did not have enthusiastic cooperation. He asked citizens to help him build a great country. But they were more interested in better living and working conditions. Soon demonstrations and strikes became commonplace again.

His next move was to try to stir up support through a public referendum. He told voters, "If you do not support me on the referendum, I will resign."

De Gaulle lost by a vote of twelve million to eleven million. At midnight on April 27, he announced, "I am ceasing to exercise my functions as President of the Republic. This decision takes effect at noon today."

The seventy-seven-year-old Charles de Gaulle continued to serve his country with eagerness.

Chapter / Ten

I Was France

The de Gaulles spent the rest of their years in retirement from public life in their home at Colombey. The man who once said, "I was France, the State, the Government" now spent his life in the roles of husband, father, and grandfather.

Flower beds in the shape of the cross of Lorraine decorated the grounds where he played with his grandchildren.

From time to time, the de Gaulles entertained their five grandchildren and dozens of grandnieces and grandnephews for dinner. De Gaulle wrote each child's name on a piece of paper. Then he had a drawing to see which children would sit by him. He liked young people, and he frequently told them: "Top students are not always those who succeed in life. Those who were well ahead of me all through school haven't been heard from since."

On rainy days, he often played solitaire or checkers with the young people, while Madame de Gaulle knitted as she watched. Sometimes they went together to the Anne de Gaulle foundation, now a home for handicapped girls.

He also finished the fourth volume of his memoirs, and he planned two more. He demanded that the house be quiet when he worked. Sometimes when his wife played the piano, he would say, "Enough, Yvonne, that's enough."

He often watched the international rugby matches on television. When France was losing, he would leave the room. His wife would call him back to watch the game if things went better for his team.

On the evening of November 9, 1970, Charles de Gaulle felt a severe chest pain. A doctor and a priest were summoned. Less than an hour later, the priest gave the last rites, and the seventy-nine-year-old general died.

Yvonne grieved, "He has suffered so much in these last two years."

As he had requested, de Gaulle was buried beside the grave of his daughter Anne. Also as he requested, no state funeral was held.

On November 12, 1970, dignitaries from all over

the world attended a Requiem Mass for de Gaulle at Notre Dame Cathedral. Hundreds of thousands of mourners marched through a heavy rain down the Champs-Elysées to the Arc de Triomphe. There they stood in silent tribute to the man who had appeared in that same place as their liberator twenty-six years before.

It is said that those who know de Gaulle either loved or despised him.

Those who loved him call him the savior of France. They praise him for being a strong and steady source of hope when France needed him most during the dark days of German occupation. They credit him for putting France on the level of the great international powers. They remember with respect his handling of the Algerian crisis, student and worker unrest, and other economic and political problems.

However, others claim that his failure to cooperate with the Allies during and after World War II hurt the French, as well as the chances for world peace. They say that the French economy and politics suffered under his strict government regulations and his refusal to work with the National Assembly. They believe that the Algerian, student, and worker crises would have been settled much sooner if he had been willing to negotiate. Finally, they criticize him for not understanding the changes that occurred during his lifetime and for never growing beyond the ideas he learned as a child.

Georges Pompidou, the next French president, said of de Gaulle: "To present-day France he gave her institutions, her independence, her place in the world."

Charles de Gaulle said of himself: "I have tried to set France upright against the end of the world. Have I failed? It will be for others to see later on."

Selected Bibliography

Apsler, Alfred, *"Vive de Gaulle."* New York: Julian Messner, 1973.

Aron, Robert, *An Explanation of de Gaulle.* New York: Harper & Row, 1966.

Ashcroft, Edward, *De Gaulle.* London: Odhams Press Limited, 1962.

Churchill, Winston, *Memoirs of the Second World War.* Boston: Houghton Mifflin Co., 1959.

Collins, Larry and Lapierre, Dominique, *Is Paris Burning?* New York: Simon and Schuster, 1965.

Cook, Don, *Charles de Gaulle.* New York: G.P. Putnam's Sons, 1983.

Crawley, Adrian, *De Gaulle.* New York: The Bobbs-Merrill Co., Inc., 1969.

Crozier, Brian, *De Gaulle.* New York: Charles Scribner's Sons, 1973.

Dank, Milton, *The French Against the French.* Philadelphia: J.B. Lippincott Co., 1974.

De Gaulle, Charles, *The Edge of the Sword.* New York: Criterion Books, 1960.

De Gaulle, Charles, *Memoirs of Hope: Renewal and Endeavor.* New York: Simon and Schuster, 1970.

De Gaulle, Charles, *The War Memoirs of Charles de Gaulle.* New York: Simon and Schuster, Inc., 1959.

De Gaulle, Charles, *The Call to Honour.* New York: The Viking Press, 1955.

Demaret, Pierre and Plume, Christian, *Target de Gaulle.* Translated by Richard Barry. New York: The Dial Press, 1975.

Eunson, Roby, *When France Was de Gaulle.* New York: Franklin Watts, Inc., 1971.

Galante, Pierre, *The General!* adapted with the assistance of Jack Miller. New York: Random House, 1968.

Lacouture, Jean, *De Gaulle.* New York: The New American Library, 1966.

Ledwidge, Bernard, *De Gaulle.* London: Weidenfeld and Nicolson, 1982.

Lester, John, *De Gaulle: King Without a Country.* New York: Hawthorne Books, Inc., 1968.

Schoenbrun, David, *The Three Lives of Charles de Gaulle.* New York: Atheneum, 1966.

Shirer, William, *The Collapse of the Third Republic.* New York: Simon and Schuster, 1969.

Werth, Alexander, *De Gaulle.* New York: Simon and Schuster, 1965.

Index